Also by John Gohorry

Squeak, Budgie! (*Smokestack Books,* 2019)

Not a Silent Night / Keine Stille Nacht - English version
of a Christmas poem, together with Bettine Koch's German
original (*Shoestring Press,* 2017)

Impromptus for George Erdmann & The Good Samaritan,
a libretto for a conjectural Abendmusik, 1705 (*Lapwing
Publications, December,* 2015)

The Age of Saturn (*Shoestring Press, March,* 2015)

Adagios on Ré - Adagios en Ré (*Lapwing Publications,* 2014)

On the Blue Cliff (*Dark Age Press,* 2012)

Samuel Johnson's Amber (*Shoestring Press,* 2010)

Forty-Eight Gates (*Dark Age Press,* 2009)

Imagining Magdeburg (*Shoestring Press,* 2007)

Talk into the Late Evening (*Peterloo,* 1992)

A Voyage Round the Moon (*Peterloo,* 1985)

JOHN GOHORRY

The
Stock Exchange
of Ideas

For Gerlinde

ARENIG PRESS

First published in 2019
by Arenig Ltd (Arenig Press)
Dolfawr, Cwmrheidol, Aberystwyth SY23 3NB

Printed in UK by
4Edge Ltd, 22 Eldon Way, Hockley SS5 4AD

A CIP record for this book
is available from the British Library

ISBN : 978-1-9998491-5-3

Cover: Circles in a circle, Wassily Kandinsky 1923

IM Fell English font digitally reproduced by Igino Marini.
www.iginomarini.com

Acknowledgements

Acumen, London Progressive Journal, The New European, The Spectator, Stand, and the following anthologies -

Junction *(Poetry ID,* 2013*)*;
From Different Skies *(Poetry ID,* 2014*)*;
Coming Into Leaf *(Poetry ID,* 2015*)*;
Paper Cuts *(Poetry ID,* 2016*)*;
Waiting for the Echo *(Poetry ID,* 2017*)*;
Loosened Threads *(Poetry ID,* 2018*)*;
'Pivotal' *Cambridge Festival of Change,* (2016*)*;
Poems for Jeremy Corbyn, *ed. Merryn Williams (Shoestring,* 2016*)*;
Strike up the Band - a Festschrift for John Lucas, *ed. Merryn Williams (Shoestring,* 2017*)*;
Write to be counted, *editors Jacci Bulman, Nicola Jackson, Kathleen Jones (Book Mill,* 2017*)*.

Armistice appeared in a special edition of The Pump, Wheathampstead and the Great War: Remembrance and Hope (*Wheathampstead History Society, November* 2018).

The headdress was shortlisted in the Bridport Poetry Competition, 2011.

Contents

The
Stock Exchange
of Ideas

As a boy, I lit fires

As a boy, I lit fires;
threw stones at windows; broke glass;
I laid bricks end to end; hid in trees;
until dusk came, I was lookout.

Tonight I'm on watch, an old man
breaking glass, lighting a small fire.
Unseen in a tree-lined city,
I lay words end to end in straight lines.

Chuang Tzu at eighty

The heart of the wise one is tranquil....

My thoughts are a flock of birds
that roost in the tree of the mind.

They squawk and quarrel, sing
when the fancy takes them, build nests

in the nesting season, pick insects
out of the air, holes in the tree.

The tree asks for silence, the green
proliferation of leaf, light and shade.

The birds keep it awake, fret it,
deny it the stillness it longs for.

Starlings

As dusk fell, the last cars
were boarding the ferry, and passengers,
no longer cramped, spread themselves in the lounge.
Headlines in English newspapers depicted
the bright, urgent landscapes of home.

I stood on the afterdeck as the sky
darkened with starlings. They rose, sank,
circled in great swarms, the shapeshifting abstract of love
perfectly formed, that, as the bow doors
clanged to, embraced the whole town.

Eight septains after Octavio Paz

(Between going and staying, 1987)

(i) *...the day wavers / in love with its own transparency.*

In the day's mirror
all your thoughts are reflected.

The small ambitions,
the small inhibitions,

the words you disliked so much,
the words you liked just a little.

The occasions you found to speak
the occasions you couldn't find,

those where you had nothing to say.
Already you're drawing up lists,

balancing your accounts.
How happy you are now, immersed

in your fable of unreflection,
in all you can't see.

(ii) .....*the circular afternoon*.....

The curve of the afternoon
sweeps towards six o'clock.

Rain falls on the decking;
the splash of a dozen pools

reflecting the ancient oak crown
still yearning for leaves to come.

Somewhere ahead lie the words
you have not yet made your own,

penned in by the early evening
as the wet laurels are penned in

by the balustrade of the decking.
You measure your life in lines

that clarify as you reach them,
dissolve on the page as night comes.

(iii) *....all is visible and all elusive....*

It slips through your fingers
like hours on a sandy beach

when the blue tide curls in,
and men prospecting for crabs

pause to admire a young woman
splashing amid the shallows

and go home empty-handed.
The wind blows a busker's music

away out of earshot, but his hands
hold his saxophone like a lover;

you'll imagine the scene for ever
though in time be unable to place it,

the photographs you'll be taking
already blurred in the album.

(iv) ....*in the shade of their names*....

The adventure park's in your head.
Someone's been dropping names;

a paper trail litters the ground
as far as the mind's eye can see.

You pursue it as best you can,
at noon reaching an olive grove

where a fellow with pencil and paper
is sheltering from the heat.

He calls you *Septimus*, welcomes you
with a few words from *A First Latin Reader:*

I lie on my back, meditate much, and write little
he says, but whether he really is Horace

or, like yourself, just an ordinary Joe
spending a day in the park, you can't tell.

(v) *....syllable of blood...*

You lie down in the Echo Room
while the cardiologist's microphone

sweeps over the gel on your chest.
The song of your blood fills the speakers,

the pulse of your life passing round
with the hiss of an ice-skater's blade,

your children, in scarves, winter coats,
powering downhill on their sledges

through a blizzard of shouts, and the tips
of the cardiologist's fingers in blue

latex gloves resting soft as snowfall
on your neck, where the carotid artery

unreels quantities of iambic so steadily
you'd have them thought inexhaustible.

(vi)...*the indifferent wall*....

You hear too much, these days, about walls,
the barriers built between nation and nation

to exclude those the builders term *aliens*.
They're made of steel, concrete, razor-wire

built on foundations of selfishness, fear,
mistrust of what's other, the acquiescence

of patriots on the inside, for whom pickaxes,
aerosols, even verses imperfect as these

bid no immigrant welcome. Nothing grows
on the wall, in the wall's shadow; security

is exclusion, refusal, and difference a scent
on a cloth guards' unmuzzled dogs strain at.

There's no other way, say the wall builders,
than building a wall to prevent terror.

(vii)...*in the middle of an eye*....

The person you most resemble
steps out onto ruined staging.

Small fires are erupting;
stone blackens, a siren wails.

The audience sit in darkness;
all eyes are on you.

You must be about to speak;
it's their expectation, and yours.

The prompt book has gone missing.
The dragon's mouth belches fire.

Who do you think you are?
Isn't this where you came in?

In the act of impersonation
you imagine you find yourself.

(viii)...*the moment scatters...*

The president's handshake
draws his visitor's hand towards him,

and greeting turns to imprisonment.
Between *have done* and *about to do*

the verb in your head is a small bird
that halts by the gardener's hand

while the *kyudoka* next door
reimagines the flight of his arrow.

Which of its thirty clues
will allow you to start on the crossword

or fly off to map the interior
of the poem that moments ago

you glimpsed as traffic lights changed
and rain came in through the skylight?

Two Chinese reflections

After Chi Lingyun

You prick your finger while sewing
and a small bloodflower blossoms.
I come from my ironing board
to comfort you with a plaster.

The clothes we hide in are watching
from hangers, the backs of chairs.
Now you frown, hunting a thimble,
a small poem scorches my heart.

After Fo-yan

When you have said you are right, who can help you?
Certainty is an oppressor.

Bang your fist on the table
and the universe comes into being.

Words fall through the sieve
where your best thoughts drizzle and shine.

Doubt sprawls in the sun,
scratches an ear with his hind leg.

Who puts out the hand of friendship
now you've finished the crossword?

The Furniture of Time

In his rocking chair, Grandfather weeps
for the biscuit that nobody brings him.

The piano where Pixie plays Mozart
prefers Barenboim, Joplin, *Chopsticks*.

What's for lunch? asks the kitchen sink.
Barley with Chicken Soup quips the stove.

A ladder climbs out of the basement
to rest on the farthest star.

The corpse in his carry cot
still calls out for lullabies.

The couple lie down in their bedroom
on a lifetime of memory foam.

The spinney

Invisible among hazels,
I lost myself in the spinney,
made up a brushwood shelter
while I was growing teeth,
learning to walk, learning balance,
learning to wear shoes.

At some stage, I went missing,
at some stage, the landscape changed.
I made hundreds of sketches,
drew maps, looking for routes
that were paved, not too steep,
safe, after dark, to be found in.

But the spinney was gone, its place
held by library, bus depot, cinema.
Who I was had gone too. In his place
was a man strange to himself
as to you now, recalling the spinney,
the paths he mapped, that went nowhere.

Proofs

(Honouring E.J. Aiton, 1920 - 1991)

A thought is an idea in transit
said Pythagoras, as the square
on the hypoteneuse proved itself
the sum of those on the other sides.

The formula holds for no power
greater than 2 declared Fermat
but my margin will not hold the proof.
Four centuries pass in the search for it.

In your classroom, the boys of 4L
and 4C baited learning with mischief;
on the blackboard, in elegant chalk,
you gave us the squeaking proof.

In transit for sixty years, our notions
of you and each other take shape
in an unfolding exchange of poems,
crystal beads, proofs of a kind.

Mound

We lived half a mile from the mound;
it lay east, over the wheatfield
we must walk round in springtime,
crawl on in the autumn for gleanings
to feed Mrs Harrison's hens.

To reach it, we left the known world
at the damson-tree stile, crossing
by ditch, footpath side, hedgerow
to where a mud track wound upwards
through nettles, thorns, briars, to the top.

The canal stretched below us, a brown
thoroughfare on the far side of a hedge.
Sometimes a barge chuntered past,
its cargo-decks freighted with coal;
sometimes a man walked a whippet

down the towpath before us; sometimes
a jay or a magpie flew. Time,
mostly, stood still. We called the mound
Pekin, because from the summit
we had a clear view of China.

The Stock Exchange of Ideas

On the *Stock Exchange of Ideas*
Originality's failing. Last month the *Index*
of Inspiration closed fifty points down
as *Dullness* continued to gain ground
and *Derivatives* rose to a new high.

Cliché did well, while *Insight*,
Wit, and *Illumination* fell through the floor.
Imitation was bullish. *Tautology*
prospered where *Brexit* meant *Brexit*
while *Greed* took *Charity* to the cleaner's.

The *Intellectual Policy Committee*
today met in emergency session.
It ruled out *Quantitative Easing*
which it said just meant more of the same
and instead proposed *Poetry Playgrounds*

- nationwide, free, and open to all
wanting to write, paint, sing, play an instrument.
In a climate of sharing, *Imagination*
would bring back former prosperity.
The project would make things happen.

Men and birds

(i) *At Shaw's Corner*

Men scuttle into their arguments. Shavian lawns
ring with the clash of dismissal, contradiction.

Not to have an opinion is to be bird brained;
not to defend it is to be caged by the enemy

who should be singing to your tune, not his own.
Mind roots in its prejudice, its vain rhetorics.

Over the writing hut thrushes flitter and sing.
Birds dart in the bushes, heedless of strong views.

(ii) *Aristophanes, Cambridge*

What is beautiful is neither human nor bird
but human as bird. In the mind's Corn Exchange

I am set free to fly by chirrupping voices,
my thoughts founding a city above the clouds

where to sing is enough, and yearning merely
that birds slim as girls in leggings and feathers

should whistle and chuck, their notes rising high
over the galleries, high above any language.

Wallace Stevens visits a makers' convention

In memoriam Jone Delahaye

At sunrise and dusk every day
a jackdaw attacks your window,
a beak-rapper, a would-be
glass-smasher, a frame-batterer
full of fury, a rat-a-tat knocker
whose voice is imperative.
Let me in, let me in he demands,
launches himself full tilt
at the glass, at the image
he has of himself, and must break,
crazy for what's inside,
whether to have or to give,
to take, as a thief breaking in
will take, or to bring, as a friend
guessing some urgent need
hurries round with a remedy.

Details of these visitations
you send with a movie attachment
from the house where you live alone
on the brow of a hill, among trees
bearing white horses and green girls
in harlequin tabards and bare feet
and where every fact is transcendent.

I sit at my desk on a warm
summer's evening, one man
in a convocation of makers.
Tonight is a night of searching,
of gathering, picking, re-working
some better-known poet's thought
into a texture that is our own.
Through open windows I hear
the murmur of passing traffic,
a car horn, the whistle of birdsong;
around me, my fellow poets
tap at their plasma screens, write
and strike out in their notebooks
as I do, or gaze into the distance

as I do, absorbed in imagining.
What they reach for, I cannot know,
the memories, musings, suggestions
they visit, pick through, leave behind
as suddenly as they came; neither
can they know what false settings out,
what fugitive images draw me down
alleyways choked by weeds, paths
leading to lifeless ponds, before
I arrive, perhaps fifty minutes ago,
in imagination at least, at your door,
and in my mind's eye, as they say,
catch sight once again of your caller.

I see him now in his sable splendour,
remorselessly other, demanding entry,
a furious clamour of beak, feet, remiges
compelling attention, engagement,
finally transformation. My confoundings
tonight are a thousand discomforts
like yours, and my hope is, given luck
and a fair wind, something of what
I imagine may in time find its way
to a language of shared discourse
round our formica-topped table
and so shape the wider world. I reach
for a window-latch, lift it up, push
the panes of the mind wide open;

there's a flurry of wings as the jackdaw
storms in and the words come, oblique,
first-, second-hand, revelatory now
that, enabled through them to frame
this invention of mine - *Poetry is
the supreme fiction, madame* - I find
myself once again reinvented,
these words my answering call
to you, to the challenge of making,
the bird's gift, enigmatic and fabulous.

To the Piraeus, 2015

How can your eyes be shut so tight and you not see me sob?
  (Yannis Ritsos, *Epitaphios*)

A man in a tattered shirt, I went down yesterday
to the Piraeus with the few coins that I had, hoping
to buy bread, cheese, fish and maybe a little wine,
but the supermarket was bare and the corner shop
where I had bought groceries for the past five years
had a sign saying *Closed for lack of trade, sorry to go.*
I asked round the neighbourhood *Where is Gregoriou?*
What has become of him? but no-one knew anything;
there was no explanation - a shrug, and a finger laid
to the lips were the only response. So I walked on
a step further and came to the old market square,
a desolate, ruined place that looked like a bombsite
with paving blocks lying everywhere and trestle tables
turned over for barricades in the last demonstration
still scattered about everywhere, the ground strewn
with spent cartridges, shell cases, canisters, car tyres.

A young woman once had a stall here selling olives,
the largest and tastiest olives, I swear, in all Greece.
Her name was Eftychia, which in English is *Happiness*;
she would stand by the tubs and sing, often giving
people who stopped by scoops of olives and feta,
and always with a smile and a song or a kind word.
Nothing remained. The doorway to the *cafenion*
where only last week I had argued with Eucris,
Pausanias, Glaucon and other budding philosophers
was a dingy space boarded with plywood, reeking
of piss, vomit and excrement; over the entrance
someone had sprayed an enormous robotic figure
armed to the teeth, the mouth of its rocket launcher
pumping banknotes into the air and the legend
I'm coming to get you beneath. I walked through

a group of abandoned shops, past an old bakery
into Prosperity Square. The banks were all closed,
their doors gated and padlocked; queues stretched
from near-empty cash machines, and the air buzzed
with ambulance sirens, the whirr of propeller blades
from overhead helicopters, the clamour of citizens
like myself who had grown desperate without means.
I turned to go home, but then caught sight of a man
whom I recognised on the steps of the National Bank.
It was my neighbour Gregoriou, sitting towards the top
of the flight, hands round his knees. He was sobbing.

I went over, put my arms round his shoulders, helped
him back to his feet. We made our way homewards.
Out in the harbour, a magnate's yacht slipped away
to the islands; in the Parliament Buildings, Theseus
rose once again to confront the Minotaur. He said
he'd *wear creditors' loathing with pride*. Gregoriou
and I picked over my last few olives, and as night fell
looked out onto the city. The Parthenon gleamed
high above us, resplendent as ever, and I thought
as always at that hour of our obligation to wisdom
and our betrayal of Pallas Athene. Around midnight
lights on the Acropolis failed, and showing Gregoriou
to his door I found the hoot of an owl gave no comfort.

Firebird IV

Looking into the fire   I see a bird in the flames
Looking into the pool   I see my face reflected
Looking into the sky   I see a cloud shifting
Looking into the ground   I see the rocks dancing.

The bird's song is a burning brand
The cloud's song is the raindrops
The song of the rocks is an earthquake
The song of my face is my mouth.

The clouds come to sit on my heart
The rocks come to pillow my head
The pool comes to dance in my throat
The bird comes to feed from my hand.

The dance of the rocks shakes the ground
The dance of the clouds sweeps the sky
The dance of the pool blurs my face
The dance of the bird frees my heart.

Eclipse

(for Dan)

From lives on our driveway
my son and I witness
celestial transformation,

the quicksilver moon
turning russet, horse chestnut
in a season of ripeness.

Side by side in our camping chairs
we celebrate being together
in a love that is not eclipsed,

our vigil tonight the confounding
of talk, age, and difference
in all we still learn from the moon.

A sackful of cloud

Two weeks ago, Mr Daldona
came with a sackful of cloud
and poured it into my left eye,
a mischievous gift that I might
make the best use I could of.

My schoolboy contemporary,
he was neither expected, nor
was he invited. I had taken him
almost a lifetime for granted,
ignored his progress, his aging.

Cloud doctors probe my gift,
arterio-cumulus analysts with
their own gifts for dispersal.
Fearful of what might occur
should cloud spread or thicken

I swallow them gladly, keep
my other eye focused on text,
atlas, keyboard, the bright bird
I can name as it sits on that forked
branch at the garden foot, singing.

At the Gorsedd Stone Circle, Porthmadog

In the act of enclosing,
a verse will leave space for your thought
to come tumbling through,
a child from the playground nearby
to jump off the roundabout
and play hide and seek in its stones.

In the echo room

I'm in the echo room, lying down
on my left side as instructed.
North, east and west of my heart
Daniela has fixed three electrodes
and now a cold gel, not unpleasant,
helps the ultrasound probe she holds
in her right hand slide over sternum,
clavicle, ribcage while with the left
she taps *allegro assai* at a keyboard.

I can't see the monitor but remember
the sweep of shadow screens years back
when my children in *utero* stirred
and the technician could tell, as I
could not, which was boy, which girl.
I remember the *lub dub* of the foetal
heart, pushing the boat body over
its whispering tidal sea towards birth
and its rendezvous with the shore.

So they landed, became adventurers,
explorers, grew to adulthood, made
and brought up their own children.
What I hear now is the splash gurgle
of my grandfather blood pushing its way
through atrium, ventricle, the open
and close of valves singing their songs
in a major or minor key while I try
to keep my boat steady, willing it

to stay out at sea for a while longer.
Thirty years back, at a friend's funeral,
one mourner read from *The Seafarer*
and his lines ring clear in my head
telling how one of three things - age,
violence, illness - sooner or later
brings every man's life to a close.
What consolation is wisdom? I ask
as my blood swishes and pumps

and Daniela's sleeve brushes my ribs
for the last time. The keyboard clatters
again and the probe's gone; she offers
wipes, reassurances, the privacy
of drawn curtains while I get back
into my shirt, cufflinks, normality.
*Doctor will contact you. Everything
looks OK. Goodbye, have a nice day.*
The door, as I go, promises closure.

Good eye, bad eye

To my good eye, he's invisible.
When I look round the room, he's not there.
When I reach for my pen, riff
through my papers, settle to write
that list or this poem, there's no sign.
I can forget he exists, and move on.

But my bad eye reveals him. He's there
in the fog and the blurry, the boy
I once was, walking the towpath
to the Colliery School, standing still
in the butterfly haunted garden,
alone on his stone by the nettlebeds

conjuring rain from a neighbour's attic.
He shifts about in the time haze,
unaware, when I call, of the old man
with the notebooks he fathered
in an East Coventry nursing home.
Seventy years have divided us,

each going his separate way; now
he brings me the gift of a bad eye
to reprove my neglect, to remind
me of my dependence, perhaps even
to show me new ways of looking,
of using the mind's eye. Pen in hand,

I return to my making. Time writes
our infirmities into her notebook in
the blink of an eye but life's too short
for complaint or for blame. Already
the neighbour's attic window bangs to,
the boy conjuring rain has run in.

Green

I cut my hand in the wood flensing apples,
bound the wound up with a dock and thought no more of it
until later a small brown crust that resembled bark
more than a scab broke through the frayed green gauze
between index finger and thumb, a third of an inch
long at first but extending slowly, and unresponsive
from the beginning to any attempt I made whether
by scratching, poking or picking to get it away.

In the palm of my hand lines deepened, multiplied
with the assurance of roots. The line of my fate
spread into a thousand deltas; my life line
diversified and unravelled so that each finger
grooved with deep fibrous strands stretched upwards
towards the clouds, towards sunlight. One day,
almost frozen to death in a snow drift, I found my whole arm,
bough-bent at the elbow, encircled with mistletoe.

My heart, once red, is now green, and these notes
that you think of as words are pure birdsong. Time,
golden and green, braids my limbs with lichen. Next year
or the year after, when the earth tilts back once again
to the sun, you'll come across me in garlands, my crown
of May blossom loud with the hum of insects, and later still,
in the months of abundance, stooping low to the ground
strewn with fallers, my gifts, ripe then, yours for the taking.

Three preludes

(i)

You woke as hands gloved in latex lifted the lid
of the autoclave and, outside, women in white
danced on the boughs of horse chestnuts.

Spotless enamel dishes rang with the clatter
of forceps; masked figures leaned and inspected.
About you were up rails and down rails.

Numbers clicked on a white wall.
You were caressed by soft hair. Honey breath
filled your nostrils with fragrance.

Shadows moved on the tiles of the ceiling.
You watched as they bloomed and faded, couldn't
make out what was said on the far side.

(ii)

At pearfall, the gardeners raked
lawn and borders with steel tines;
the bruised fruit bled where they cut.

You hid in your tree and rehearsed
your magpie clamour, your wasp drone;
about you the orchard stood firm.

Far off, the house emptied its rooms
of what it had hoarded - books,
furniture, treasure chests, children.

The gardeners advanced, gathering
moss they had raked into green sacks.
Their big boots made scuffs on the lawn.

(iii)

You lay in your bath and remembered
the afternoon, fifty years gone, when you fell
like a stone among Avon swans.

The cold currents hugged. You breathed
water until the hand of the man you loved
reached over the gunwale, and pulled.

Now widowed, you looked at your teeth
in their dish by the taps, and sank deeper
into the pineforest freshness. Its fragrance

was not that of care homes, hospital wards.
Rain drummed on the bathroom window,
filled the pit he'd dug by the poplars.

The headdress

The professor, before he retired, would put on
shorts, trainers, running vest, and run out
over the back fields at lunchtime for an hour,
or for two hours, if lecturing schedules allowed.

He ran, thinking of nothing; or rather, he ran
so that he should think of nothing, letting go
even of wanting to let go all the pedagogue
facts that were still utterly vital, the dull

rivalries, chores he knew no longer mattered.
One day, he picked up the jet black feather
a rook had let fall in a wheelrut; another day
brought him the cinder grey plume of a heron

blown from a stream. Other days added more.
He kept them at work in a drawer, looked
then for farm twine and found it by gateposts,
made himself first a chaplet, later a headdress

he hid in a hollow tree, ran by on a modified
circuit, picked up, wore and set down again,
a garment that he knew certified his becoming
a new, bird-running self. He did not wear it

on his big day of speeches and presentations
and some years afterwards, finding it stuffed
into an old jar at the end of a bookshelf, bundled
it out into recycling. But ever after reflected

on the time talk became birdsong; wisdom,
the broad flight of mind above circumstance;
learning, the loss of oneself in another,
and true happiness, being a bird.

Other

When Other moved in next door
I heard what I took for chants
in a jabber that made no sense,
saw him in his headscarf,
the comedy pantaloons
that boasted of difference

as he set out in the morning
to take over some British Job.
He disregarded the flag
I flew from my house front
and when *The Fraternity* called
locked his door, turned his lights off.

*

But when *The Brotherhood* broke
into my house, and set fire
to all I held precious, it was Other
who rescued me from the flames,
gave me clothes, food, comfort,
a room in his own house.

He taught me the language
of kindness, compassion,
helped me rebuild my home.
Now Other and I are good friends.
I'm ashamed of my prejudice;
I'm flying a different flag.

My neighbour's house

My neighbour's house is on fire
- what on earth can have caused it?

A candle left unattended?
A frying pan left on the cooker? Bad wiring?

Was it carelessness? Arson?
Petrol poured through his letterbox?

Was it visitors? Burglars? Relatives?
Friends? Fire raisers? Houseguests?

Was he storing inflammable liquids?
Ammonium nitrate? Aerosols?

And what's he done to deserve this
now his house has burned down?

What will he do? How live?
Where will he find a home?

These are just some of the questions
police will want answered

now I call Fire and Rescue
seeing smoke under my own stairs.

Solitude

Together, they wrote a book.
Its title was *Solitude*, or
Every Man his own Hermit.

They wrote alternate chapters
in a small room with one chair and a desk
hardly bigger than A4.

Bip wrote on Saturdays, Mondays
and Wednesdays, Bop on the other days.
On Sundays, neither wrote.

On Sundays, they went together
to search for the stuff of fiction.
They travelled, gambled, dug gardens,

dated deep women, whose talk
they would agonise over on weekdays
at that desk, working out meanings.

Dolmen

Time has weathered stone
and water collects in gulleys
of her own making. In flooded rock
a drowned snail decomposes.

The larger capstone
weighs thirty tons, the smaller twenty.
On the question of *how*
sits the stone fact of *is*.

There's no call here
for music or words.
The wind on the stone suffices.
The great stones themselves are glyph.

Did those who lay here
imagine the fall of stone,
their own dissolution
the tribe's extinction?

A green beetle hovers
within reach of our hands
and a lizard deceives our eyes
between stone and shadow.

Four thousand years
are the blink of a lizard's eye;
and time herself is this breeze
that the stones cannot capture.

A platform of words

We're on a platform of words
once part of Antarctica.
It towers over three miles high,
only a ninth of it visible,
and our history's written
in its permafrost lexicon
deep under our snowshoes.

It has survived since the first
word refracted its meanings
for the woman who whispered it
into the ancestor's ear, the drip
of his icicle heart falling like seeds
to sprout in the soil below,
where mosses unmultiplied

since the beginning of time
broke from their brood bodies
to speak the language of green.
We've held it together for half
a lifetime with treaties and small
acts of kindness performed
when not much was at stake,

mapping the limits of discourse
in the hope that cold currents
swirling about the pole would keep
the scream of whale song alive,
the vernaculars of the pod
plunging hundreds of fathoms
down to subglacial lakes

the fabled meltwater of comets.
But the continent has been fractured
by commerce and exploitation;
the atmosphere overheats,
the sea warms, and ice groans
as the prospector's drill cuts in.
The language of coexistence

with its lexis of nurture, respect,
restraint, above all, has given place
to acquisition's imperative,
the thunder of ice cliffs falling
into the sea overwhelming
the cries of auk, petrel and tern
on their desperate searches

for food, and the floe broken
adrift from its moorings
shrinking visibly by the hour
as the land masses belch carbon,
the seas rise and what once
was a continent dissolves
in apocalypse, and we drown.

What should we sing of now?
When ice is a memory, how
should we celebrate prudence,
how practise love, wisdom,
stewardship for the future?
What poetry shall we make
out of gurgle and suffocate?

What's to become of us?
How will our children live?
Can we reverse the meltrate,
look with leviathan's eye,
learn to cherish the cold?
Is there still time? Is there will?
Still a chance of survival?

You sit on the back row

You sit on the back row
watching the action unravel

 - a child at a border fence
blinded by tear gas,

a dictator, ninety-two now, partying on
in his drought-ridden dictatorship,

the seismic aftershocks
of an underground atomic explosion,

a massacre in a high school,
starvation, rapes, torture, beheadings.

On stage, public speaking
is an art of deception,

the candidates in the roadshow
building walls with their rhetoric,

and party smears all that's on offer
to purge our dystopias.

The Senecan pageant rolls on,
its bloodthirsty improvisations

remorseless as clockwork;
the roadshow antagonists deliver

the lines they have learned by heart.
It must all run its course, you think,

nothing can change it now.
Except you, in the darkness,

free to stay, free to leave,
can exercise freedom of thought,

and now the lights come on
leave your seat on the back row,

walk out into the street, into
the rest of your life and there,

resolute in the hurl of traffic,
make all the difference you can.

Have with you to Savile Row, or, A Pleasant Satire of A Son's Wardrobe Packed with his Mother's Wisdom, newly brought up out of Witney in Oxfordshire and despatched on Wednesday last to Islington North.

Clothes make the man
that's what my mother says,
and it's known for a truth
throughout the civilised world.
So in that scruffy jacket
can we be the same species?
In those baggy, creased trousers
can you be truly human?

       Put on a proper suit.

You can trust a man with a tie
that's what my mother says
and it's known for a truth
throughout the civilised world.
So what do you call that
piece of cloth round your collar?
Are you Slipknot or Windsor?
Tell-Truth or Tell-a-Lie?

       Do up your tie.

Words are the dress of thought
that's what my mother says
and it's known for a truth
throughout the civilised world.
So what are you thinking of,
keeping Mum when the band
strikes up our six patriot notes?
Fill your lungs full of air,

       sing the national anthem.

When the argument's lost,
get the man, say the orators,
and no-one recalls, for now,
how you shafted my argument.
So when the progressives come
in beards, trainers and torn jeans
I'll straighten my tie, shoot a cuff,
and, quoting my mother, tell them

            No need to get personal.

Settlements

The man hunting buffalo
on the Icknield Way grasslands
had no concept of garden,
school, nursery, substation.

He knew cooking pot, spear tip,
the sweep of ground from the hill,
the movement of stars he named
in a tongue old as aurochs.

Driving along in trousers
past Redhoods and Archers Way
I imagine his pale ghost
trekking the chalkhill furlongs

in search of something to kill,
eat, keep the settlement strong.
But three thousand years have passed,
and long since, they engulfed him.

I wait at a traffic light
where they're repairing the road;
what would he make of white lines,
marks on the ground for passing?

I imagine him gored by mammoths
in Morrisons car park, bear
hugged in a garage forecourt,
and drive on, to my future.

At sea

It's calm tonight on Dover Beach,
gulls punctuate the strand;
the Border Force maintain their watch
over our moon-blanched land.

Somewhere out there in flimsy craft
a rumoured migrant host
makes progress through the trafficked waves
towards the English coast.

The latest bulletins announce
what Government advice is;
the urgent steps it has in hand
to circumvent a crisis

- high level talks with France, to prove
the land of dreams illusion,
a second cutter on patrol
to reinforce exclusion.

Meanwhile in Ramsgate phantom ships
assembled in the docks
will transport lorryloads of goods
safely past phantom rocks.

Contingent planning makes its mark,
and seals on prudent grounds
a small commission, to the tune
of fourteen million pounds.

On Dover strand alone we stand,
unwelcoming and free;
along the coast our proudest boast
a government at sea.

Sappho returns to Letchworth

Who was it, beautiful votress of Aphrodite,
that came to you in the dead of a May night
and waking no-one in the nearby houses
raided the garden

rich with the scent of blossom where you rested,
and not only stole your heart, but carried off
all of you, body and soul, and the Greek lyre
you melted hearts with?

I wonder sometimes whether it might have been
a posse of the beautiful, bold, gay girls
you loved and wrote verses for - long-legged Arctis,
Atthis, whose eyebrows

were two crescent moons, Pathia honey-tongued,
strange-cadenced Rhodopis, Phyllis, all sunlight,
Anactoria, with the buttery lips
and eyes to die for.

Outraged to see you neglected, forgotten
by many, did they on the wings of passion
spirit you back to Lesbos, offering there
true veneration?

I wish it were so, but more likely it was
rough men, scrap metal merchants lusting for bronze,
who drove up from Luton or the Elephant
in a low loader,

burned you off your pedestal with blowtorches,
tied you to the bed of their truck with strong cords
and before dawn had broken in Foundry Street
had melted you down

and sold you for what you would fetch. May you
haunt their wives' dreams for ever and may women
of all persuasions, seeing what they are, turn
from them in disdain!

But today you return to the garden, cast
in a new mould, with fresh robes, and a new lyre
tuned already for singing. It's time to dance,
time for rejoicing.

It's a new century and a new era;
let your music bring joy to our hearts, your words
speak of love's anguish as always, and this time
we'll be attentive.

Rhodopis to Sappho

In Cairo, men paid me to dance
in a tunic painted with palm trees
and sandals laced to the knee;

they fed me the filthy script
I spoke that they took for love lines
and paid me when it was over.

But here in Lesbos you take me
unwashed, with thorns in my feet,
bruised ribs, and lice in my hair;

you anoint me with honey, speak
tender words in my ear, and your lips
touching mine, ask no payment.

Whistleblower

He's on line to the Houyhnhnms,
Swift's horses that cannot lie;
from their stalls in the Pentagon,
in the Kremlin, in Whitehall,
they send him the documents
the state would keep secret

- the evidence of its frauds,
treacheries, tyrannies, the crimes
it has carried out undercover,
unsuspected of until now,
the conspiracies it has not yet
enacted, still at the planning stage.

He resolves their encryptions,
frets over meaning, significance;
stir crazy, spends hours pumping
iron in his weights room, boxes
with shadows, shadows of shadows;
goes out after dark to leak data

to men in underground car parks
who have contacts in newsrooms.
Going home, heedful of footfalls
on the opposite pavement,
he takes three different buses,
checks stairwell, lift, vigibox,

the sellotape strip on his front door
for signs of intruders, enters.
The balcony window is closed
just as he left it, the talcum dust
on the hologram of himself
fingerprint free, undisturbed.

A letter from Lesbos

When you left us for England
we waved you goodbye
from the harbour at Mytilene
and returned to our lovers
in the aniseed beds of Eresos.

Inclusive, permissive,
we embodied your teaching
in our welcoming arms;
our shames were intolerance,
pride, whatever withheld love.

We got on with our lives,
played music, wrote verses,
sang hymns to the power of love
in the waterside restaurants,
all the heart's thoroughfares.

Our life of pollen and lightning
might have lasted for ever
had not Homer's Aegean
cast up neither Greeks nor Trojans
but Syrians, Kurds, Iraquis

- men, women, children, babies
in arms, migrants all, refugees
by the hundreds, the thousands
crammed in unseaworthy boats
from their war-torn cities, hungry,

exhausted, cold, wanting shelter,
somewhere to rebuild a life.
We remembered our vows and brought
round-the-clock medicine, blankets,
food, shoes and clothing to a shore

piled with punctured inflatables,
lifejackets, the tarpaulin shrouds
of the drowned, helped survivors
make their way to the mainland,
to England, perhaps, and safety.

In a thousand years, mistress,
may whoever remembers Lesbos
remember our acts of mercy
and Syrian songs in England
praise all our island is famed for.

Seven Sea Studies *(after John Greening)*

(i)

Childhood - the chafe of sandgrits, the quarrels
of those enormous bad-tempered birds they call *seagulls*;
the shuffle of red and brown crabs glimpsed in rock pools
as the cabbage-field of the waves blusters and spills.

(ii)

The moon is magnetic. It pulls the sea up and up,
puckers salt water to wave, can't hold on, lets it drop.
Whence the tide. It folds over, flooding towards your foot.
You stand where it curls, barking orders like King Canute.

(iii)

Slim girls in shrieking thongs dance through the shallow-splash;
you swim a few lazy strokes, eyes on that darkening patch
at the Wagnerian horizon where fate warns that love will fail.
Yseult's boat comes drifting towards you under her black sail.

(iv)

You're Mum and Dad suddenly. Eight children eager for rides,
and spades; later on, Vettriano suits, jackets and ties,
white stones for back home, midnight harbour-wall vanities,
wisdom, love, laughter; grief; the treacheries of the tide.

(v)

A grounded man now, you've found somewhere to escape
the toad work, fix those caesuras, get your verses in shape;
you pack your mouth full of pebbles, dumb as Demosthenes,
and discover at last your own rhetoric. Or the sea's.

(vi)

Walking's harder, these days. You can get *down* from cliff
-top to shingle well enough, but coming back *up* it's as if
you've a mountain to climb. Soon, you can't move an inch,
glad of height, distance, perspective, a pensioner's bench.

(vii)

In the epoch of *sans*, sands fall through your hourglass mind;
the beaches are quicksand but helping hands not unkind.
Red and brown creatures shuffle about in rock pools
pestered by birds you think might be called *seagulls*.

Armistice

White flares over no-man's land
turn men to shadow;
the dull thump of mortars

robs the living of life.
The shadow they have become
is brought with flags lowered

through coils of barbed wire
to the poppyfield present
where grieving-grateful

we stand at our Menin Gates
as the Last Post is sounded
proclaiming our lesson learned.

Fabrics

In the Noh play, *The Lady Aoi*,
she herself is a strip of red cloth.

The cufflinks that Ferret wears
to write sonnets in are faux pearl.

Lady Gaga appears on stage
in a dress made of beef cuts.

The fabric of gravity shakes
as black holes jostle each other.

Ferret's verse is opaque,
composed wholly of dark matter.

ARENIG PRESS
Dolfawr
Cwmrheidol
Aberystwyth
Ceredigion
SY23 3NB

www.arenig.co.uk